THE SONGS OF
CHRISTMAS
By Bill and Gloria Gaither

FOREWORD

Christmas is such a rich, momentous environment for making memories. Every year as we experience family gatherings, special trips, wonderful aromas unique to this season, parties, pageants, and remember loved ones who have passed, and cherish loved ones who are present, our reminiscences of Christmas are increased and enriched. And let us not forget that wonderful thread that weaves its way through so many aspects of our Christmas celebrations past and present… SONGS.

Bill and Gloria Gaither, two of our most beloved Christian writers and musicians have created and compiled an exquisite collection of Christmas songs that have become an integral part of our personal and collective Christmas memories. These are songs that will rekindle the warmth of Christmases past. These are songs that will wreath our joy of Christmas present. These are songs that will be a treasured part of Christmases to come.

May your Christmas be rich in memories – overflowing with thanksgiving, and filled with comfort and joy!

BETHLEHEM...GALILEE...GETHSEMANE

Words by
WILLIAM J. GAITHER and GLORIA GAITHER

Music by
WILLIAM J. GAITHER

Gentle ballad ♩ = 66

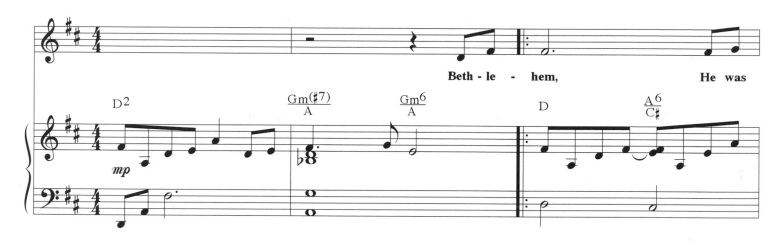

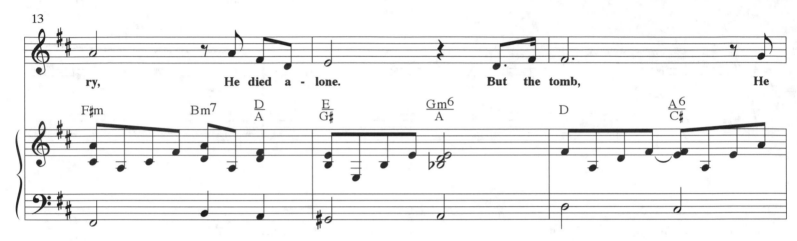

BRING BACK THE GLORY

Words by
GLORIA GAITHER

Music by
WILLIAM J. GAITHER
and BILL GEORGE

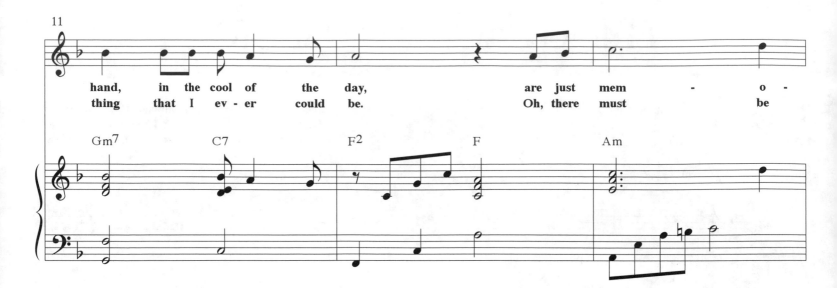

hand, in the cool of the day, are just mem - o -
thing that I ev - er could be. Oh, there must be

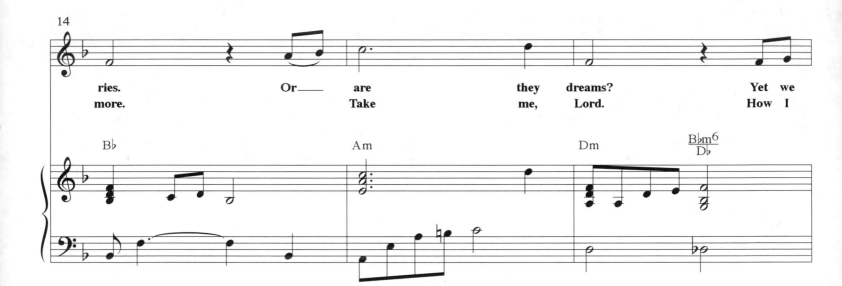

ries. Or____ are they dreams? Yet we
more. Take me, Lord. How I

hold to the hope that the mu - sic will come back a - gain.
need you to give me a glimpse of e - ter - ni - ty.

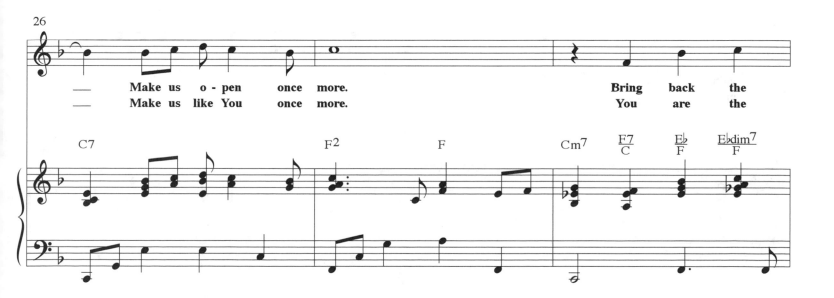

mu - sic,   the trust,   the won - der   that's just like   a   child   who has nev - er   known
mu - sic,   the trust,   the won - der   that's just like   a   child   who has nev - er   known

pain.   Bring back   the glo - ry,   the glo - ry⎯⎯⎯ a -
pain.   You are   the glo - ry,   the glo - ry⎯⎯⎯ a -

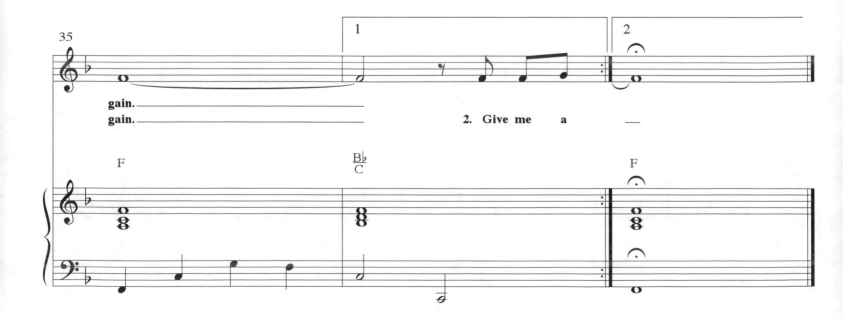

gain.⎯⎯⎯
gain.⎯⎯⎯   2. Give me   a ⎯

CHANGED BY A BABY BOY

Words by
GLORIA GAITHER and
BENJAMIN GAITHER

Music by
BENJAMIN GAITHER

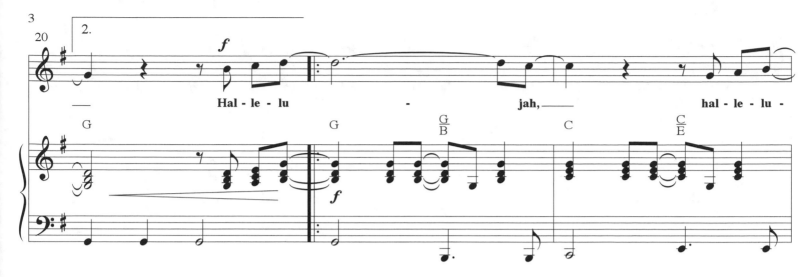

ba - by boy. No mat - ter how long__ and no mat - ter how far, their

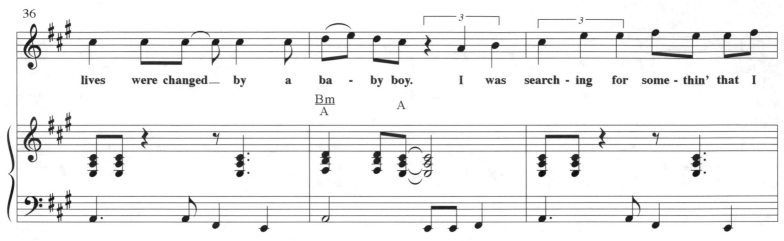

lives were changed__ by a ba - by boy. I was search - ing for some - thin' that I

could not name__ un - til my life was changed__ by a ba - by boy. I gave Him room__

__ and I__ am not the same,__ be - cause my life was changed__ by a

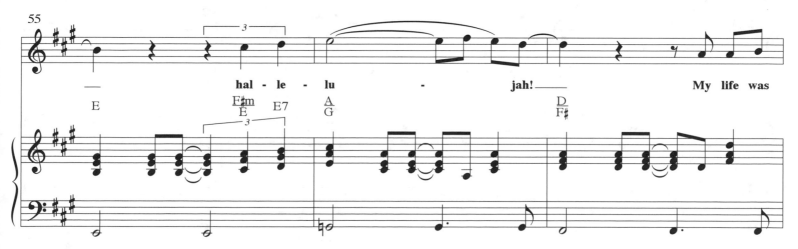

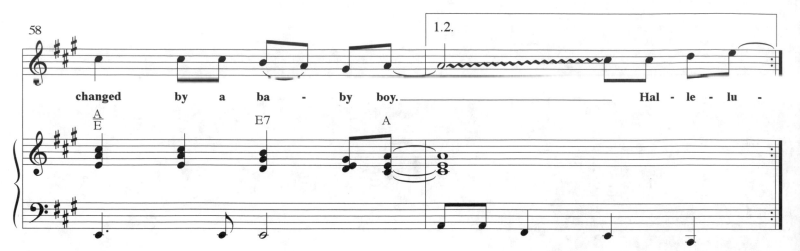

changed by a ba - by boy. _____ Hal - le - lu -

_____ Hal - le - lu - jah! _____ My life was

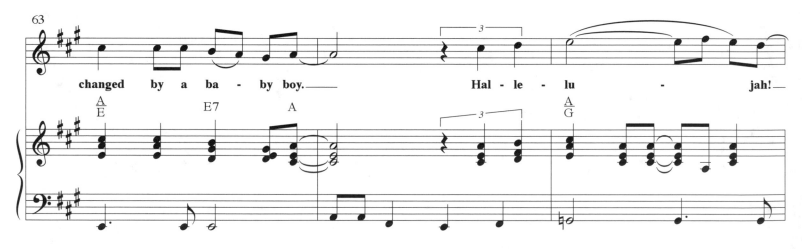

changed by a ba - by boy. _____ Hal - le - lu - jah!

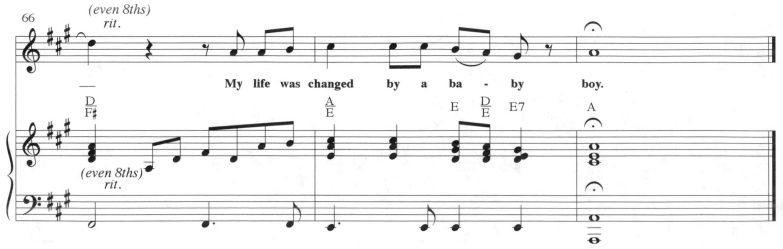

_____ My life was changed by a ba - by boy.

CHRISTMAS IN THE COUNTRY

Words by
GLORIA GAITHER

Music by
WILLIAM J. GAITHER, MICHAEL SYKES
and WOODY WRIGHT

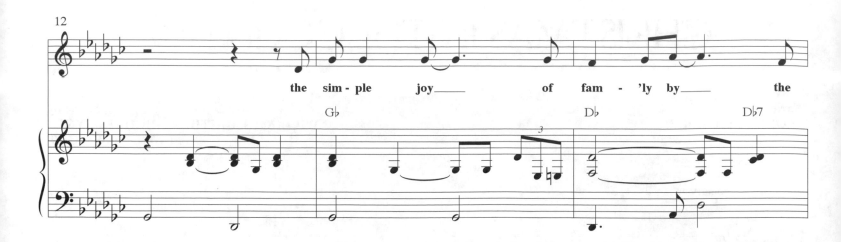

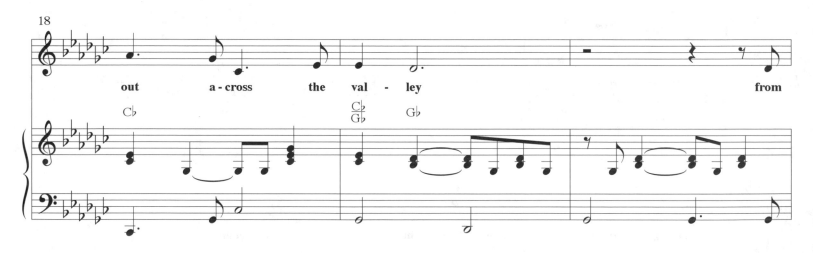

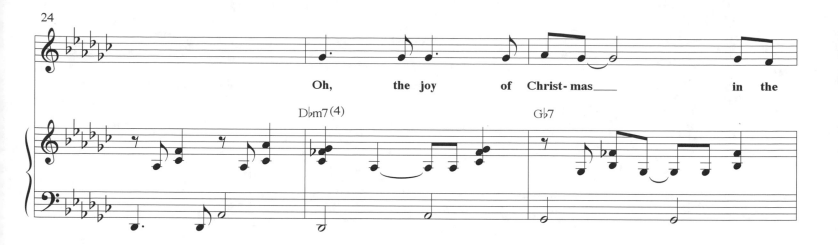

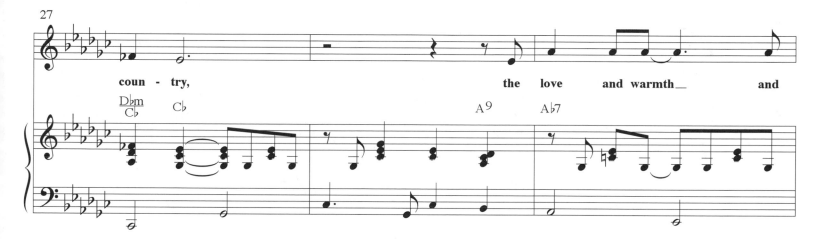

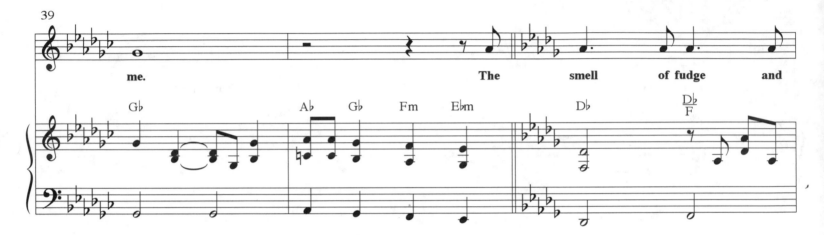

the whis- pered sounds___ of se - crets___ from the___

___ chil - dren___ em - brace and call___ back

home the likes___ of me.___ There's

noth - ing quite___ like Christ - mas in the coun - try,

when si - lent snow____ is fall - ing on____ the

barn. And chil - dren press____ their

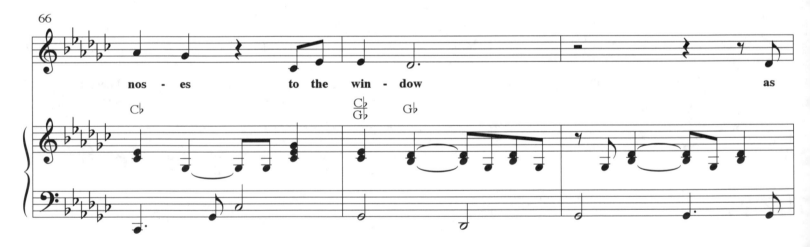

nos - es to the win - dow as

win - ter turns____ to mag - ic the old farm.

That's the joy of Christ- mas_____ in the

coun - try, the love and warmth_____ and

gen - tle mem - o - ries and

know-ing that_____ the sim - ple, old love_____ sto - ry_____

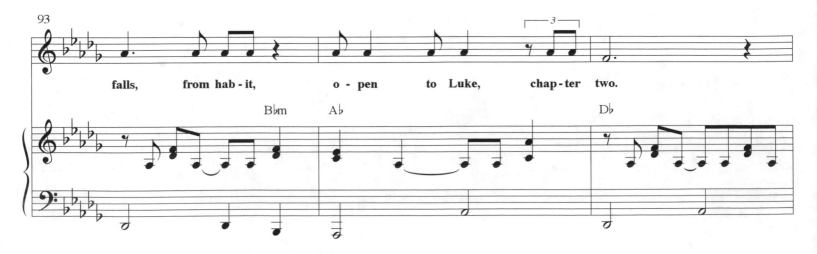

And none of us will ev - er tire of

hear - ing,_____ "Now chil - dren, here____ is

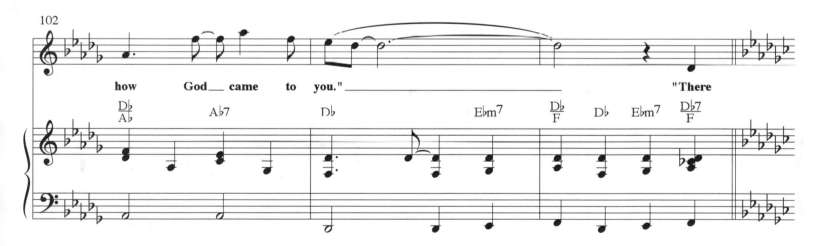

how God__ came to you."_____ "There

were, in that__ same coun - try, shep - herds watch - ing

the flocks at night____ up - on a lone - ly

hill..." And with his well - worn

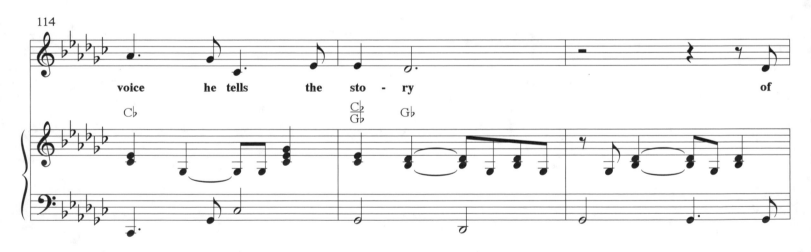

voice he tells the sto - ry of

how God loved_ us once and loves us still.

COME AND SEE WHAT'S HAPPENIN'

Words by
GLORIA GAITHER

Music by
WILLIAM J. GAITHER, WOODY WRIGHT
and MICHAEL SYKES

Come and see___ what's hap-p'nin' in the barn!___

I've seen noth-in' like___ this since I've___ been on___ this farm! Those

cho - rus, "You'll find the new Mes - si - ah o - ver there!"

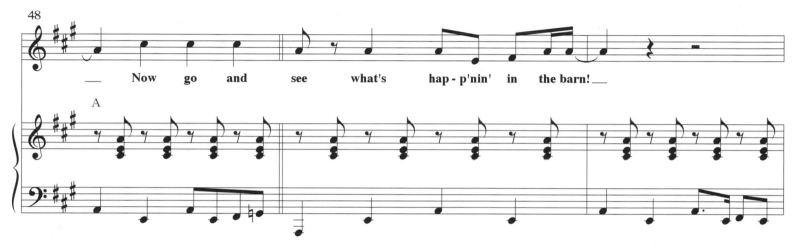

___ Now go and see what's hap - p'nin' in the barn! ___

There's been noth - in' like ___ it ev - er hap - pen on ___ this farm! Those

stran - gers camp - in' out ___ there have a Ba - by in their arms. ___

Come and see____ what's hap - p'nin' in the barn!____

p growing as you go

Come and see,____ come and see,____ come and see_

____ what's hap - p'nin' in the barn! Come and see,____ come and see,

come and see!_____

GLORY IN THE HIGHEST

Words by
GLORIA GAITHER

Music by
WILLIAM J. GAITHER, BILL GEORGE
and BILLY SMILEY

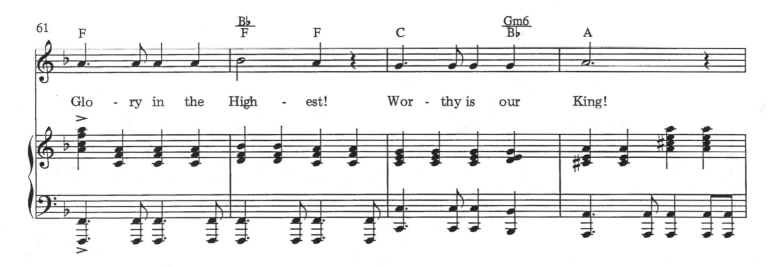

HE STARTED THE WHOLE WORLD SINGING

Words by
GLORIA GAITHER

Music by
WILLIAM J. GAITHER and
CHRIS WATERS

HE'S STILL THE KING OF KINGS

Words by
WILLIAM J. and GLORIA GAITHER

Music by
WILLIAM J. GAITHER

1. In the hills of Ju - de - a the lone shep-herds watch; Hope is gone, there is no call for sing - ing;_____

walked by the grave - sides of earth's fall - en kings, Who op - posed Him and yet He's still reign - ing!_____

rode thro' the ci - ty, the crowd claimed Him King; Thou-sands cheered and the streets filled with sing - ing;_____

sound of the trum - pet, the skies blaze with fire; Moun-tains thun - der with God's judg - ment sing - ing;_____

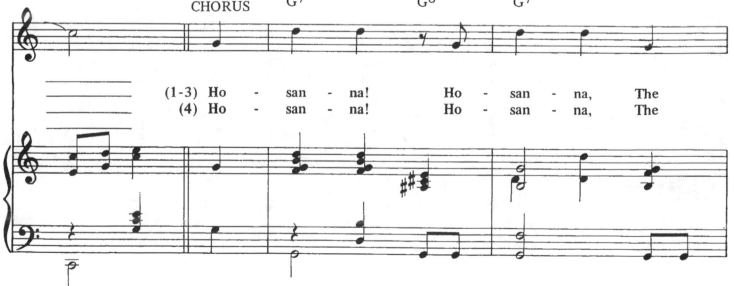

IT'S A TIME FOR JOY

Words by
GLORIA GAITHER

Music by
WILLIAM J. GAITHER, MICHAEL SYKES
and WOODY WRIGHT

With great joy! ♩ = 120

It's a time for sing-in', it's a time for friends, __ a time for wrap-pin pack-ag - es to send. It's a time for hug-gin' ev - 'ry-

start - ed with an an - gel, It start - ed with a
can - dles in the win - dow, the car - ols in the

star, it start - ed with a sta - ble, as -
snow, the gifts that say, "I love you," the

trol - o - gers who'd trav - eled far. It start - ed with some
star - lights' gen - tle glow, the fire that warms my

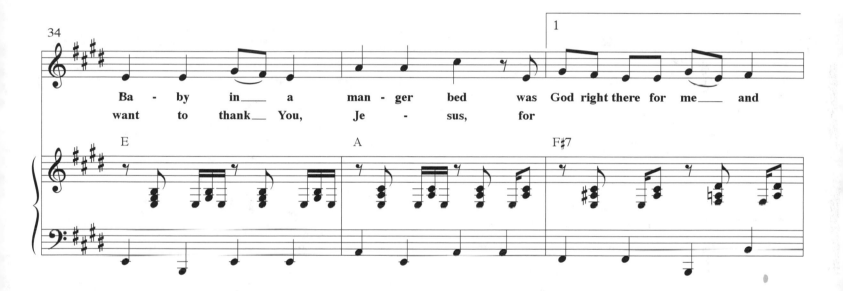

time for sing in', it's a time for friends, a time for wrap - pin' pack - ag -

es to send. It's a time for hug - gin' ev - 'ry -

one you meet, a time for bak - in' all their fa - v'rite treats. It's a

time for se - crets no one knows but___ you, a time for fam - i - ly and

neigh - bors, too. A time for chil - dren, a time for toys, ___ but

most - ly it's a time for joy! It's a time for chil - dren, a

time for toys, but most - ly it's a time for joy! _____

IT'S CHRISTMAS

Words by
GLORIA GAITHER
and GERON DAVIS

Music by
GERON DAVIS

With a lilt ♩. = ca. 65

Sil - ver bells___ jin - gle and lights start to twin - kle— It's Christ-mas!

Snow - flakes are fall - ing and friends come a'- call - ing— It's

Christ - mas! Car - ol - ers___ sing - ing and

church bells are ring-ing, they're wish-ing us all hope and cheer. The

reds and the greens___ paint a ho-li-day___ scene and it tells us that Christ-mas is

here!_____

Store win-dows spar-kle, the trees in the park say, "It's Christ-mas!"

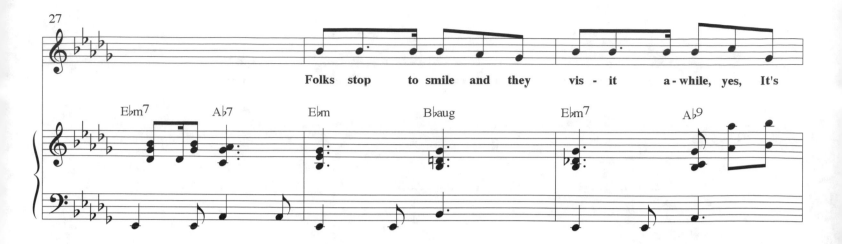

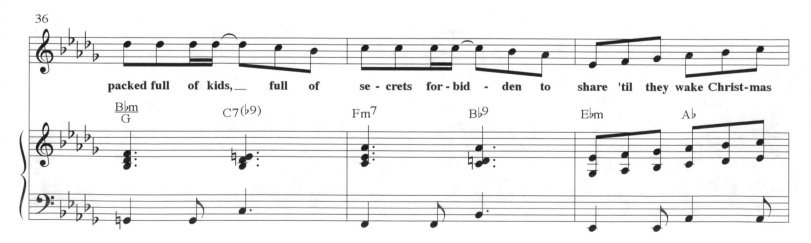

day._____ There's no hap - pi - er

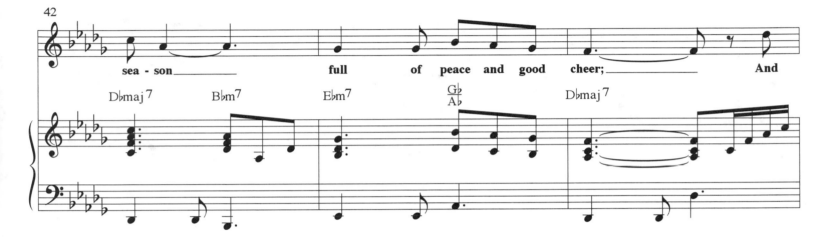

sea - son_____ full of peace and good cheer;_____ And

there's a ver - y good rea - son:_____ God came to live with us

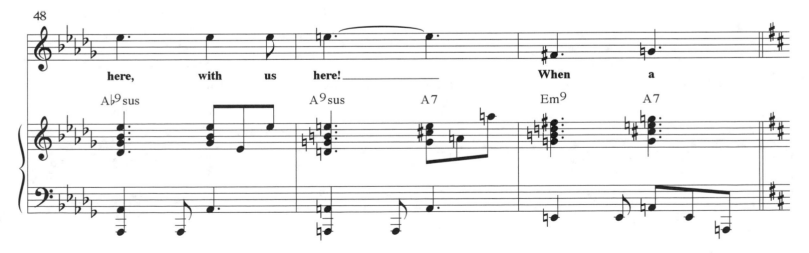

here, with us here!_____ When a

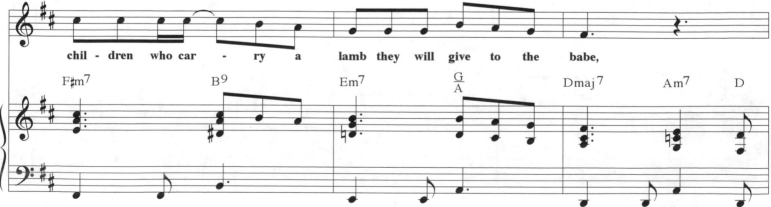

Wrapped up in swad - ling clothes– as ev - 'ry-bod - y knows– this means that it's Christ-mas

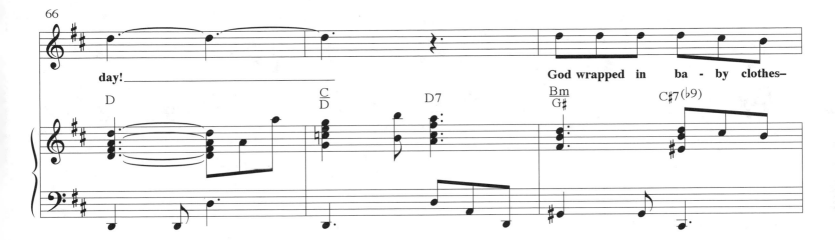

day!_____ God wrapped in ba - by clothes–

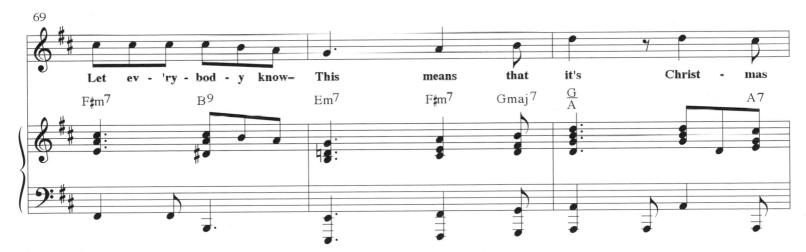

Let ev - 'ry-bod - y know– This means that it's Christ - mas

Day!_____ It's Christ-mas!

IT'S STILL THE GREATEST STORY EVER TOLD

Words by
GLORIA GAITHER

Music by
WILLIAM J. GAITHER
and J. D. MILLER

hold.   A tax law_____ and a jour-

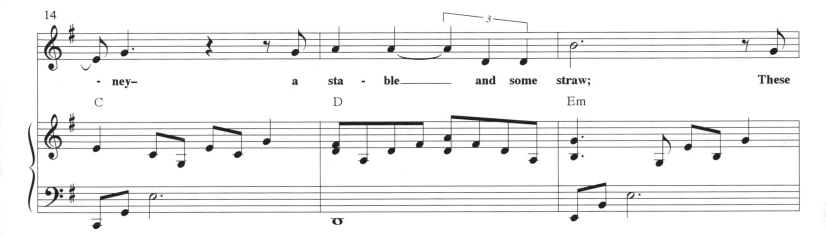

-ney—   a sta - ble_____ and some straw;   These

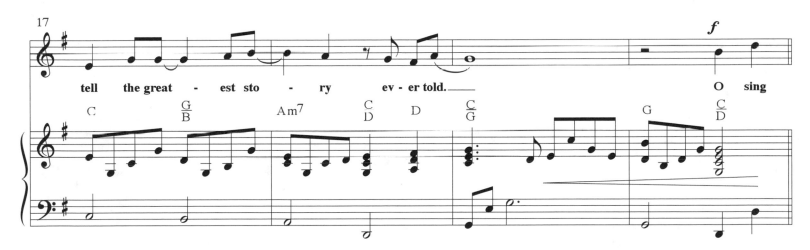

tell the great - est sto - ry ev - er told._____   O sing

glo - ry in the high - est—   He is come,   our great   Mes -

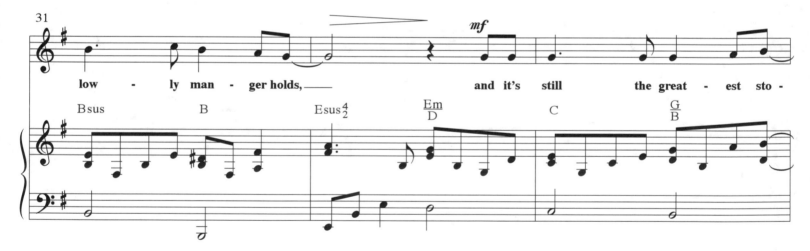

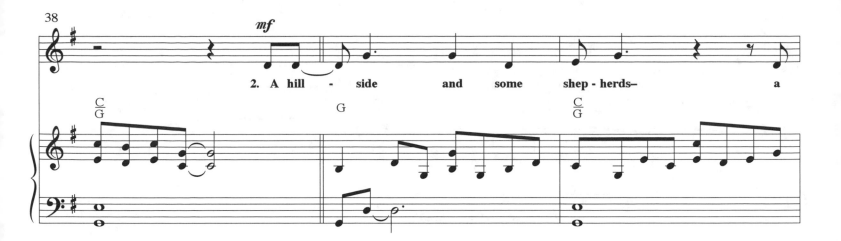

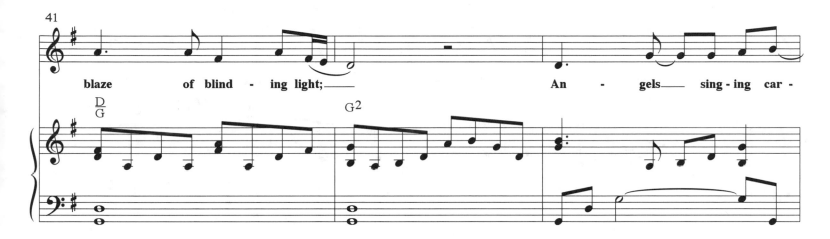

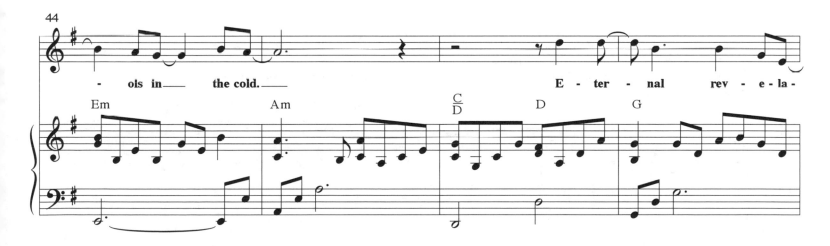

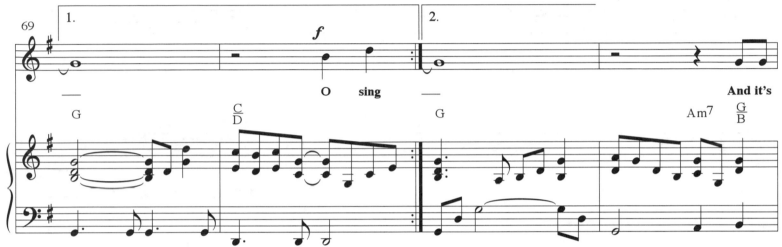

JESUS, WHAT A LOVELY NAME

Words by
GLORIA GAITHER

Music by
WILLIAM J. GAITHER

Je - sus; It's such a love - ly name.
make us one, And Je - sus is His name.

Da - vid's throne———— Reign-ing o - ver
Joy re - stored!———— While a heart pierced

Ja - cob's home———— For the Glo - ry now has come And
by the sword———— Gives birth to a ris - en Lord, And

Je - sus is His name.————
Je - sus is His name.————

LISTEN TO THE ANGELS SINGING

Words by
GLORIA GAITHER

Music by
WILLIAM J. GAITHER, MICHAEL SYKES
and WOODY WRIGHT

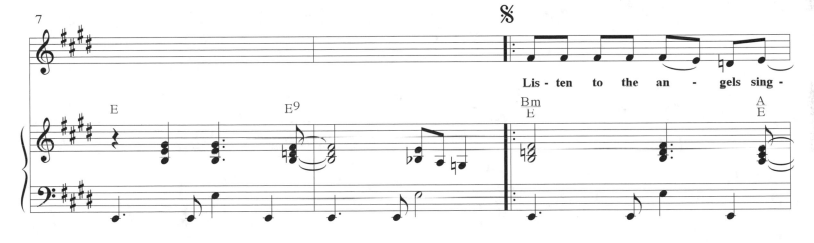

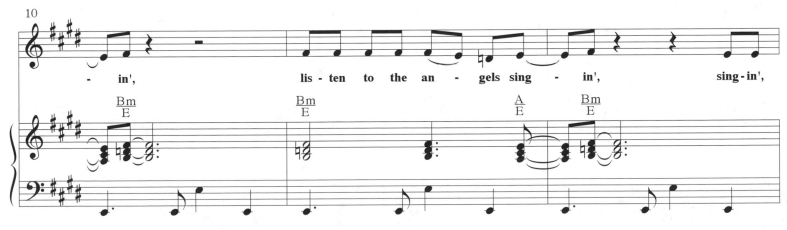

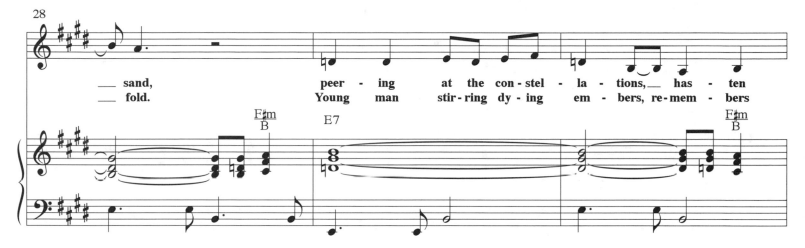

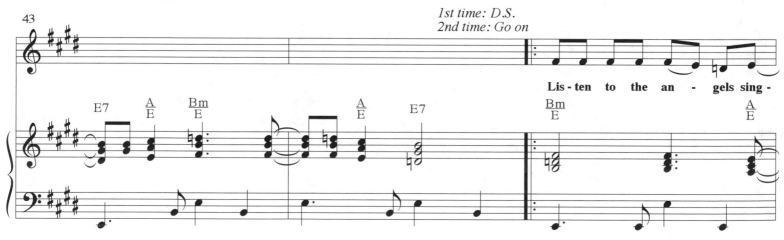

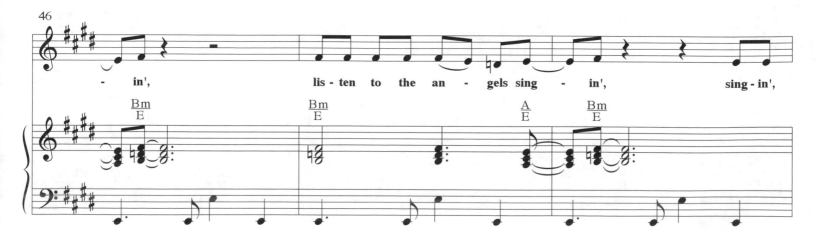

"Glo - ri - a!"_____ "Glo - ri - a!"_____

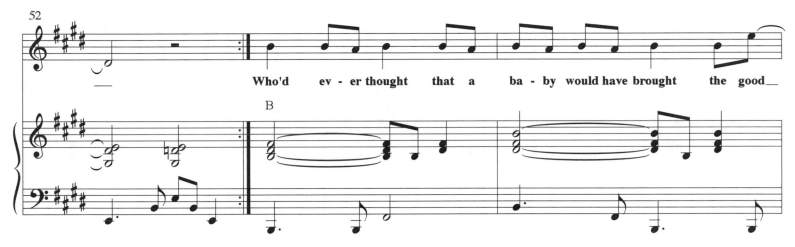

___ Who'd ev - er thought that a ba - by would have brought the good___

___ news?___ Hear the an - gels sing - in'!_____

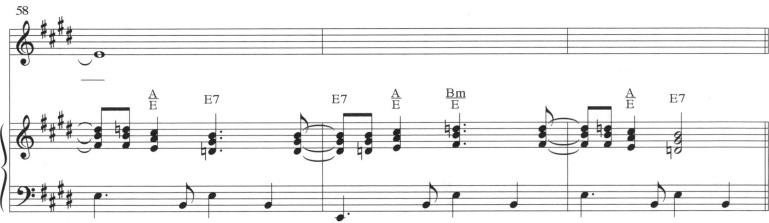

Lis - ten to the an - gels sing - in', lis - ten to the an - gels sing -

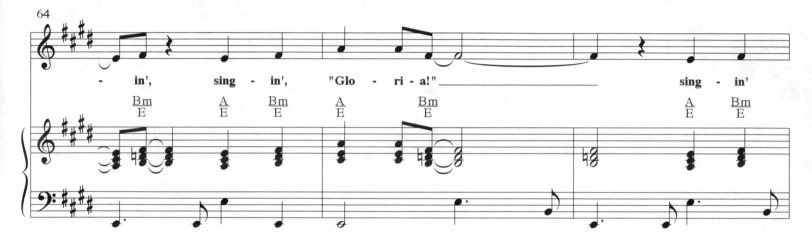

- in', sing - in', "Glo - ri - a!" _____ sing - in'

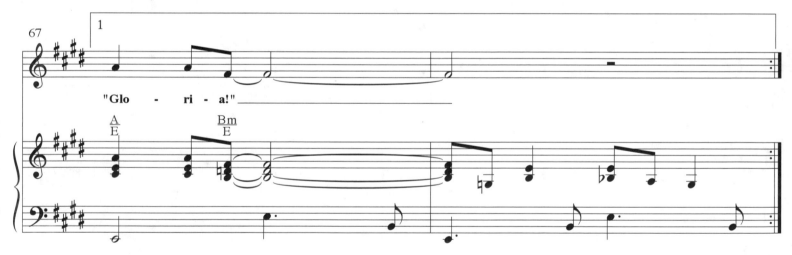

"Glo - ri - a!" _____

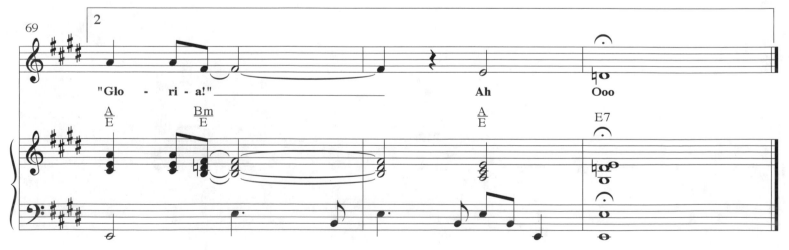

"Glo - ri - a!" _____ Ah   Ooo

MARY WAS THE FIRST ONE
TO CARRY THE GOSPEL

Words by
MARK LOWRY

Music by
WILLIAM J. GAITHER

Mar - y was the first one to car - ry the gos - pel when the an-gels brought the news of that pre - cious lit - tle boy. Mar-

MARY'S SONG

Luke 1:46-50

Adapted by
GLORIA GAITHER

Music by
WILLIAM J. GAITHER
and BILL GEORGE

MY FATHER'S ANGELS

Words by
**WILLIAM J. and
GLORIA GAITHER**

Music by
DONY McGUIRE

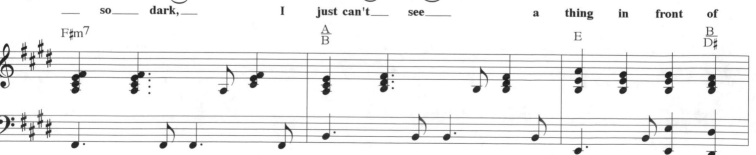

MY HEART WOULD BE YOUR BETHLEHEM

Words by
GLORIA GAITHER

Music by
WILLIAM J. GAITHER
and J.D. MILLER

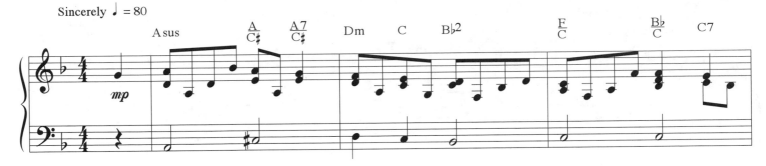

1. My heart would be Your Beth - le - hem, a shel - ter for Your birth; My bod - y be Your
will would bow in won - der - ment, struck si - lent by the awe Of an - gels vis - i -
mind would make a pil - grim - age wher - ev - er prom - ise shines, Il - lum - i - nate e -

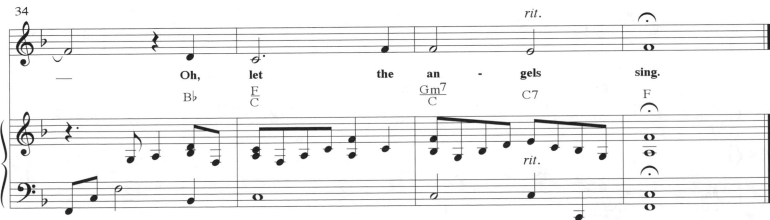

REACHING

Words by
WILLIAM J. and GLORIA GAITHER

Music by
WILLIAM J. GAITHER

mind,_____ And the Word of the

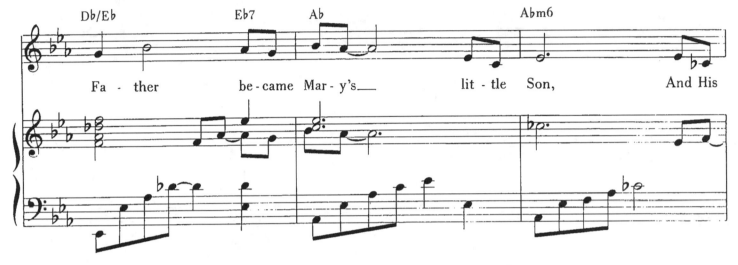

Fa - ther be - came Mar - y's____ lit - tle Son, And His

love_____ reached all the way_____ to where I was._____

Last time to Coda ⊕

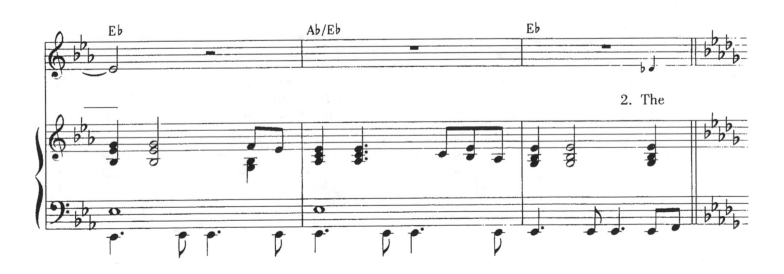

2. The

REDEEMING LOVE

Words by
GLORIA GAITHER

Music by
WILLIAM J. GAITHER

1. From God's Hea-ven to a man-ger From great rich-es to the poor
2. (From a) lov-ing Heav'n-ly Fa-ther To a world that knew Him not

Came the Son of God to seek and save; From the
Came the "Man of Sor-rows," Christ the Lord; In my

a-zure halls of Heav-en To a rough and rug-ged cross, Je-sus came and
wan-der-ing He found me Bought my soul with His own blood, Gave to me a

98

REJOICE, THE GLORY HAS COME TO US

(optional a cappella)

Words by
GLORIA GAITHER

Music by
BILL GEORGE
and MARK LAYCOCK

THE SENDER AND THE SENT

Words by
GLORIA GAITHER

Music by
GERON DAVIS

time   and space   He____ went;   the ba - by who had

Gm7   A7(♯5)   A7   Dm7   Fm   F2sus Fm6

al - ways been   the Send - er and   the Sent.

C/E   F2   Dm7 Dm9 G7sus G7   C2   Fm   Fm2 Fm

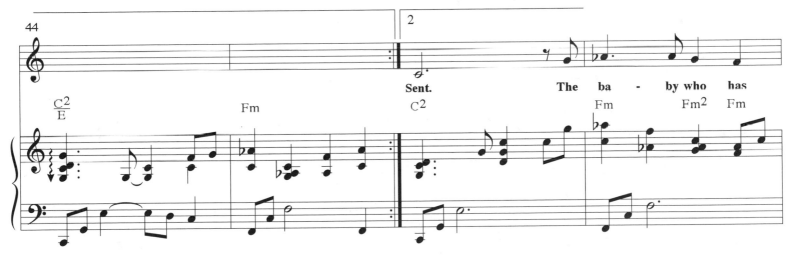

Sent.   The ba - by who has

C2/E   Fm   C2   Fm   Fm2 Fm

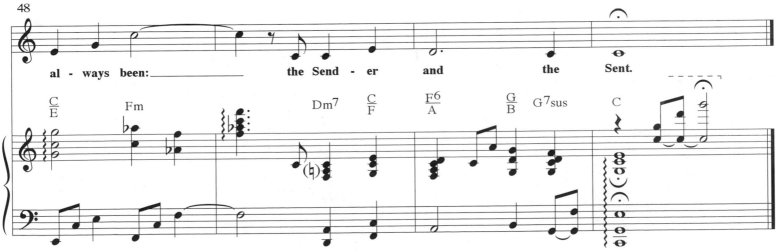

al - ways been:____   the Send - er and   the   Sent.

C/E   Fm   Dm7 C/F   F6/A   G/B G7sus   C

SHEPHERD'S SONG

Words by
GLORIA GAITHER

Music by
WILLIAM J. GAITHER

SHEPHERD (Medium/High Voice)

Mu- sic?_____ Do I hear mu- sic?_____

Could there be mu - sic,_____ Or am I get - ting

old? Yet I thought I heard a song._____

MESSIAH IS BORN/Smiley-Gaither

SHEPHERD'S SONG/Gaither

27 sing - ing?_____ The night is so dark_____ and cold. How__

A♭/E♭   B♭9

31 could there be a song?_____

a tempo (pulsing four)

B♭m9   B♭m7/E♭   A♭2

a tempo (pulsing four)

MESSIAH IS BORN/Smiley-Gaither
CHOIR/WORSHIP TEAM

35 To the town,___ the town of Beth - le - hem!

A♭   Fm   D♭   E♭   D♭/E♭   E♭

39 We must go_____ and wor - ship Him!

A♭   Fm   Fm/A♭   B♭m   E♭

SHEPHERD'S SONG/Gaither

MESSIAH IS BORN/Smiley-Gaither
CHOIR/WORSHIP TEAM

SHEPHERD'S SONG/Gaither
Shepherd Solo

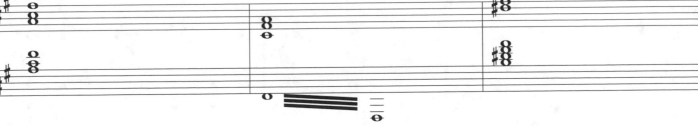

f Mu - sic!_____

Him!_____

Suddenly Slower

A♭ A²

Yes! I heard mu - sic!_____ There can be

A aug

mu - sic..._____ I'm not just hear - ing

F♯m/A   F♯m   B⁹

SILENT COMES THE JOY

Words by
GLORIA GAITHER

Music by
WILLIAM J. GAITHER
and JEFF KENNEDY

Slow and gentle ♩ = 80

Si - lent comes the joy
joy
joy

with - out proud an - nounce - ment,
de - liv - ered to a man - ger,
like a spring e - rup - ting,

Like the hint of
In the qui - et
Un - seen in the

glo - - rious—
dream - - - ing
tell - - - ing

her - ald - ing the day.
that sin had torn a - way.
the pow'r of the un - seen.

B

B7

E

1, 2

3

2. Si-lent comes the
3. Si-lent comes the

Si - lent comes the joy,_____

A²

—— si - lent comes the joy._____

F♯m⁷

A/B

E²

TONIGHT!

**Words by
GLORIA GAITHER**

**Music by
BENJAMIN GAITHER**

Rhythmically, in four

Kings and shep - herds make___ their way___ straight to where___ the ba - by lay,___

rich and poor___ and lone - ly   bow be - fore___ this sight.___   A

star has   led   them   to   this place.___   The Word_

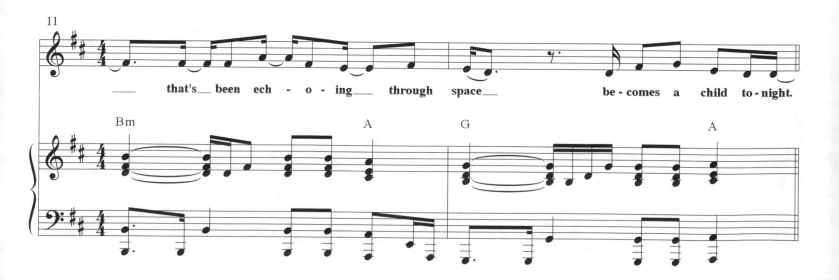

___ that's___ been ech - o - ing___ through space___   be - comes a   child to - night.

Star to mark__ the Mes- si - ah's__birth; Star of heav - en now touch - es earth to-night.

An - gel voic - es fill__ the air,__ an - gel wings__ are ev - 'ry - where.__

Light so bright— it's blind - ing, shep - herds shake— with fright. "A

warmth be - gins to flood the hill.———— "Fear not!—

Peace to you,— good - will," — comes to earth to - night.

D.S. al CODA 𝄋

WE BEHELD HIS GLORY

Words by
GLORIA GAITHER

Music by
WILLIAM J. GAITHER and **J.D. MILLER**

1. The Word that spoke worlds in-to ex-ist-ence, the Word that bro't or-der and plan, That di-vid-ed the light in-to dark-ness, breathed life in-to dust that was man; The
2. The Word that was Al-pha, O-me-ga, Ya-wah, Je-ho-vah, Shad-dai, The Word that shat-tered the moun-tain and carved out of stone "I Am I;" The

Word   that span - gled the heav - ens   with   gal - ax - ies flung in - to
hope   that rang thru the a - ges   God's   prom - ise to A - bra-

space,   This   Word came to dwell a - mong___ us   to tell the
ham,   The   seed - ling that sprang from the des - ert   be-came the

glo - ry of God___ and His grace.   And we be - held   His
glo - ry, the Word in flesh, a - live!

rall.   a tempo

glo - ry,   yes, we be - held the glo - ry,   the

in - car - na - tion sto - ry, the Word in flesh a-

live! And we be-held His glo - ry, a

child be - comes the sto - ry, And love be -

came a - live.

D.C. once

D.C. once

INDEX

Product Information

Vocal Folio 797242851490

(Available from your favorite music supplier or Word Music.)
For more information on Gaither products, contact your favorite
music supplier, Spring House at 800-955-8746 or Gaither.com.